Tales of Nature Lost among the Thorns

Silent writer and Jaydin C Donough

Published by Jaydin Donough, 2024.

Table of Contents
Copyright
Dedication
Acknowledgements
About the Author
Foreword
Chapters
Chapter 1: The Bud (New Love)
Chapter 2: Full Bloom (Deep Love)
Chapter 3: Thorns Appear (Challenges in Love)
Chapter 4: Falling Petals (The End of Love / Letting Go
Chapter 5: Rebirth (Healing and New Beginnings)
Chapter 6: Traditional Love
Chapter 7: Modern Love
Chapter 8: Spiritual Love (Transcendence)
Final Sections
Epilogue
Notes
Final Words / Closing Message
Glossary

Copyright © 2024

All rights reserved. No part of this book may be reproduced, stored in a retrieval system, or transmitted in any form or by any means—electronic, mechanical, photocopying, recording, or otherwise—without the prior written permission of the publisher, except for the use of brief quotations in a book review or scholarly journal.

This is a work of fiction and poetry. Names, characters, places, and incidents either are the product of the author's imagination or are used fictitiously. Any resemblance to actual persons, living or dead, events, or locales is entirely coincidental.

Published by: Self published Jaydin C Donough

Also by Silent writer

Tales of Nature Lost among the Thorns

Watch for more at www.wattpad.

Also by Jaydin C Donough

Please Don't Forget About Me Tea For My Soul
Tales of Nature Lost among the Thorns

Dedication

For those who have loved, lost, and found themselves again.
To the ones who held on through the thorns and let go with grace.
And to the hearts who find beauty in the struggle, joy in the pain, and the strength to bloom once more.

Acknowledgements

No creative journey is ever truly solitary, and I owe my deepest thanks to those who made this book possible.

To my family, for their unwavering support and belief in me, even when I doubted myself.

To my friends, who offered their patience and kindness as I navigated this complex exploration of love, constantly encouraging me to follow my heart and write fearlessly.

To the poets who have come before me—your words laid the foundation upon which I've built this work. Your insight into the beauty and pain of the human heart has inspired every page.

To my editor and team, for their tireless efforts in helping to shape this book into its final form. Your dedication to the craft has been invaluable.

Lastly, to every reader who finds themselves within these pages—thank you. It is for you that I write, in hopes that my words may comfort, inspire, or simply remind you that you are never alone on your journey of love.

About the Author

Jaydin Donough is a poet and writer whose work delves into the intricacies of love, loss, and renewal. With a deep appreciation for both traditional and modern forms of poetry, Jaydin brings a unique voice to the exploration of the human experience, drawing on nature, spirituality, and personal growth as key themes.

Jaydin was born and raised in Hazendal, Athlone in Cape Town, where he cultivated a love for words at an early age. Inspired by the works of poets like William Shakespeare, Sylvia Plath ,Emily Dickinson, Ella Wilcox, and many more poets, his writing often combines rich imagery with emotional depth, inviting readers to reflect on their own journeys of the heart.

When not writing, Jaydin enjoys gaming, music and reading and exploring the natural beauty of Cape Town. This is his third published collection of poetry.

Foreword

The nature of love is both eternal and ever-changing—a paradox that poets have long sought to capture through the written word. In Tales of Nature Lost Among the Thorns, [Your Name] takes us on a journey through the stages of love, where beauty and pain, joy and sorrow, are inseparable parts of the human experience.

Love, much like the roses that grace the cover of this book, is delicate, vibrant, and often accompanied by thorns. Through carefully crafted verses, this collection invites the reader to explore the fullness of love: from the tender moments of early romance to the bittersweet reality of loss, and the eventual renewal that comes with healing.

What makes this collection so unique is its balance between traditional poetic forms and the raw honesty of modern love. [Your Name] seamlessly blends the classic beauty of sonnets and villanelles with the free-flowing expression of modern poetry, ensuring that each piece resonates with readers on a deeply personal level.

More than a simple exploration of romantic love, these poems reflect the spiritual, societal, and self-reflective aspects of love. They remind us that love is not confined to a single definition; it is a living, breathing entity that grows, fades, and transforms over time. It is in the thorns that we find our resilience, and in the bloom that we find our joy.

This collection is for anyone who has ever loved, lost, and found themselves again. It is a testament to the power of the human heart to endure, and ultimately, to bloom once more.

Enjoy the journey.

Jaydin C Donough

Chapter 1: The Bud (New Love)

"Love is like a young, tender shoot—beautiful in its frailty, powerful in its potential."
~~Jaydin Donough

A Bud of Spring

In early bloom, you are a soft caress,
A tender bud upon the vine of time.
With every word, your voice brings tenderness,
A growing warmth that climbs in subtle rhyme.
The sky blushes in hues of softest pink,
As petals, trembling, stretch toward the sun.
In your embrace, my heart begins to drink,
The morning dew—this love has just begun.
Yet fragile is the bloom before it grows,
And careful hands must guide the tender stem.
Though thorns may hide beneath the sweetest rose,
I'll hold it close and learn to cherish them.
For love in bud must gently start to show,
Before its petals fully start to grow.

Blush of Dawn

A blush of dawn upon your cheek,
Your smile, a light I long to hold.
The breeze that dances through the peak,
Is warm, yet whispers soft and cold.
The sky turns soft, a rose-lit hue,
With streaks of amber through the gray.
And standing close, I look at you,
As shadows gently slip away.

Soft Gazes

Your eyes are windows into something new,
A world where words no longer need their place.
The stars are waking, painting skies deep blue,
Their light reflected softly on your face.
We stand beneath a canopy of trees,
The scent of jasmine wafts upon the air.
Your gaze, like moonlight, sets my heart at ease,
And in that moment, nothing else is there.
The way you look at me—it speaks of hope,
A budding dream of what we soon might share.
Like vines that twist along a gentle slope,
Our love grows slowly, with both time and care.
So let me drink it in, these fleeting hours,
For soon the bud will bloom, and petals fall.

TALES OF NATURE LOST AMONG THE THORNS

New Beginnings

A gentle hand, a soft hello,
The spark of something new.
We walk through fields where flowers grow,
As petals brush with dew.

Hearts Entwined
(Couplet)

Two hearts entwined in early spring,
Like swaying trees where robins sing.

Garden of Wonder

In the garden of wonder, we plant our first seed,
With hands full of dreams, in no rush to succeed.
The soil is soft, as warm rain starts to fall,
Each droplet a promise—our love standing tall.
We wander through blossoms of lavender skies,
With petals like whispers, soft kisses on eyes.
The scent of fresh earth, the hum of the trees,
A symphony played by the wind and the breeze.
And here in this garden, with hearts open wide,
We trust in the bloom that our love will provide.
In the warmth of the sun, we rest in its light,
For in every bud, love's beauty takes flight.

First Glance

I caught your glance across the room,
A spark that set the air alight.
The evening sky began to bloom,
As day turned softly into night.
The world around us paused and slowed,
Like petals falling on the breeze.
Your eyes a language all their own,
A silent call that whispered, "Please."

TALES OF NATURE LOST AMONG THE THORNS

Touch of Spring

Your hand in mine, a fragile thing,
Like leaves just born from winter's grasp.
We walk the path where robins sing,
And every breeze is love's soft gasp.
The trees above are flushed with green,
Each branch a cradle for the sun.
And in your touch, new life is seen,
As love begins its quiet run.
The river hums, the air is still,
But here beneath the canopy,
I feel the stir, the subtle thrill,
That blooms between both you and me.
So as we walk, with love so young,
I know our song has just begun.

Dew on Petals

In morning light, I found you near,
A rose with petals soft and new.
Though beauty's touch may cause me fear,
I reached to hold the bloom of you.

TALES OF NATURE LOST AMONG THE THORNS

Beneath the Blossoms

Beneath the blossoms' gentle sway,
We whisper dreams in softest tones.
The world, for now, seems far away,
And all we have is what we've grown.

The First Step

We took the first step, hand in hand,
Unspoken love, like grains of sand.

Morning Dew

The morning dew upon the leaves,
Like soft confessions still unsaid.
And though the heart so often grieves,
New love begins where hope is fed.

A Secret Smile

I caught your smile beneath the sun,
A secret only you and I could know.
And in that moment, life was spun
From threads that only new love can sew.

Love's First Light

Love's first light is soft,
It creeps in slowly,
Like dawn rising across a sleepy horizon.
At first, you don't notice—
But soon,
Everything is painted in its glow.
And before you know it,
The world is bright,
And you wonder how you lived without it.

The Sweetest Bloom

In every glance, I see the tender bloom,
A flower born from nothing but the sun.
And though we walk through silence, through the gloom,
I know that love, once started, can't be done.
For love is patient in its quiet state,
It grows with time, with care, with whispered grace.
And though the world around us hesitates,
I see our love reflected in your face.
So let it bloom, this love that we have grown,
With roots that stretch beyond what eyes can see.
For even if this love must stand alone,
It blossoms with the sweetest kind of plea.
And when it blooms, the world will know our name,
For love, once born, will never be the same.

Chapter 2: Full Bloom (Deep Love)

Opening Quote:
"When love blooms, it does so in layers—each petal revealing a deeper beauty, a richer story."
~~Jaydin Donough

In Full Bloom

In full bloom, our love is like the rose,
Its petals deep with passion, velvet red.
Each touch of yours, like sunlight, gently flows,
And I, within your warmth, feel wholly fed.
We dance beneath the open sky, the breeze
A lover's sigh that whispers through the trees.
Your laughter lifts me, carries me with ease,
As flowers bend and sway in tender pleas.
The earth beneath our feet feels soft and warm,
A cradle for the life our love sustains.
And even when the winds become a storm,
This garden grows untouched by fear or rains.
For love, when rooted deep within the soul,
Will bloom, despite the world beyond control.

TALES OF NATURE LOST AMONG THE THORNS

Of Wine and Honey

Oh, how sweet is the love we share,
Like wine pressed from the ripest fruit,
A golden nectar beyond compare,
That runs through veins and roots.
We taste the honey of each kiss,
Each sip a richer, sweeter bliss.
Your touch, like silken threads, entwines,
Binding our hearts in secret signs.
In the evening light, we sit and drink,
Our hands like vines that gently link.
No words are needed in this space,
For in your eyes, I see my place.

A Garden Grown

In every glance, a thousand flowers bloom,
Each petal soft, unfolding in your gaze.
Our love, like gardens, fills the empty room,
Where once was only shadow's quiet haze.
You are the rain that soothes the thirsty earth,
The sunlight that awakens every tree.
And through your love, my heart has found its worth,
A forest grown where barren land would be.
So take my hand, and lead me through this place,
Where love is woven thick as ivy green.
With every step, we leave behind a trace,
Of life renewed, of beauty yet unseen.
For love, like nature, knows no end or start,
It blooms forever deep within the heart.

Whispers in the Dark

In the still of the night, when the world fades away,
And the stars are but whispers that light up the gray,
I find you beside me, your breath on my skin,
As love's quiet symphony softly begins.
The room is a cocoon, a velvet embrace,
With shadows that dance, tracing lines on your face.
No sound but the heartbeat we share in this space,
Where the night hums with love's endless grace.

Love's Depths

Love's depths are like the ocean, wide and vast,
With currents that we cannot hope to see.
Beneath the surface, treasures hold fast,
A secret world for only you and me.
We dive into this sea of endless blue,
Where every wave is richer than the last.
No fear resides within this love so true,
Our hearts are anchors, holding firm and fast.
And even when the storms around us roar,
We sink into the quiet, peaceful deep.
For in the ocean's heart, there is no war—
Just love that waits in silence as we sleep.

TALES OF NATURE LOST AMONG THE THORNS

The Sweetness of Silence

In silence we find love's sweetest call,
For words, though sweet, can't say it all.

Heartstrings in Harmony

Our hearts beat in perfect tune,
A melody played in the light of the moon.
Each chord you strike, I feel within,
As love's sweet music softly begins.
Your touch is the note that holds me still,
A song in the air, a warmth to fill.
And though no words may pass our lips,
Our love is the song that gently grips.

TALES OF NATURE LOST AMONG THE THORNS

The Dance of Us

We dance beneath the canopy of stars,
A rhythm only we can feel and know.
Your hand in mine, we twirl through earthly bars,
Unseen by all, where only love can go.
The night is ours, a stage of silver light,
Each step a pulse, our hearts the steady beat.
The world dissolves, and in this sacred night,
We move as one, our love a dance complete.
The trees above sway gently with our song,
The wind a chorus to our tender sway.
In you I've found the place where I belong,
A partner through the night and every day.
So hold me close, and let the stars bear witness,
For love is in the dance, a quiet stillness.

Light Between the Leaves

The sunlight filters through the leaves,
And paints your face with gold.
We sit beneath the quiet trees,
As love's soft stories unfold.

TALES OF NATURE LOST AMONG THE THORNS

Heart's Harvest

In love's embrace, we find our ground,
A harvest ripe beneath the sun.
Each whispered word, a joyful sound,
Our hearts entwined, our souls as one.

The Depths of You

I dive into the depths of you,
Where light fades to shadow
And silence is thick as the ocean's floor.
In this quiet, I find the beauty,
The hidden colors that only I see—
Not in the glow of day,
But in the softness of the dark.
You are the mystery I dare to know,
The endless sea where my heart feels whole.

In Love's Light

Your light is warm upon my face,
A gentle sun in love's embrace.
It lifts me up, it holds me near,
And melts away my every fear.
I close my eyes and feel you there,
A glow that dances through the air.
For love, like this, is soft and true,
A warmth that guides me back to you.

A Garden Grown Together

Together we have grown this garden, love,
Each flower bright beneath the sunlit sky.
Your laughter blooms, my voice the wind above,
Our days like petals, drifting soft and high.
And though the seasons change, our roots are strong,
They sink into the soil of earth and time.
We weather storms, for here is where we belong,
A garden grown in harmony and rhyme.

The Lasting Bloom

This bloom we share, it grows with steady grace,
A love that weathers every turn and test.
Though time may change its form, it leaves a trace,
A constant warmth held tight within the chest.
For love that's true will shift, and bend, and sway,
Like branches heavy in the autumn light.
But never will it drift too far away,
Or lose its brilliance in the softest night.
So let us hold this lasting bloom, my dear,
And trust in all the beauty it will bring.
For love, once grown, will never disappear,
But rise again with every breath of spring.

Chapter 3: Thorns Appear (Challenges in Love)

Opening Quote:
"Love is a rose that blooms with thorns—beautiful, but never without pain."
~~Jaydin Donough

The Thorn's Sting

The rose we hold is wrapped in thorns so tight,
Its petals blush with pain we cannot see.
What once was love is lost in endless night.
We reach for beauty, crave its fleeting light,
But in our hands, the blood begins to be.
The rose we hold is wrapped in thorns so tight.
The tender bloom now wilts beneath our sight,
We squeeze too hard, our love, no longer free.
What once was love is lost in endless night.
We cannot blame the rose for its fierce bite,
It grew with thorns, protecting destiny.
The rose we hold is wrapped in thorns so tight.
Our hearts now struggle in their desperate fight,
The beauty fades, the pain our only plea.
What once was love is lost in endless night.
And yet we hold it still, despite the fright,
For love was once the bloom we longed to see.
The rose we hold is wrapped in thorns so tight,
What once was love is lost in endless night.

Words Like Thorns

Your words, like thorns, have pierced me deep,
And though I bleed, I will not cry.
They fester in the wounds I keep,
Each whispered line a quiet lie.
The petals fall, the color fades,
Our garden now is overgrown.
And where there once was sunlight's rays,

TALES OF NATURE LOST AMONG THE THORNS

Now only thorns, alone, are shown.

Frayed Threads

The threads of love are frayed, too thin to hold,
Each tug we make tears deeper than before.
What once was warm is now too dark, too cold.
We wove our lives together, brave and bold,
But now our hands are raw from pulling more.
The threads of love are frayed, too thin to hold.
The knots we tied with promises grow old,
Each twist now burns, no longer we restore.
What once was warm is now too dark, too cold.
Our whispered words no longer ring with gold,
Instead, they fall to silence at the door.
The threads of love are frayed, too thin to hold.
And though we try, our hopes have turned to mold,
The fibers snap, the life we built now tore.
What once was warm is now too dark, too cold.
Perhaps we stay out of fear of the fold,
But in the end, we're empty at the core.
The threads of love are frayed, too thin to hold,
What once was warm is now too dark, too cold.

Shattered Silence

The silence stretches long between our breaths,
A chasm wide and deep where words should live.
We stare at walls, at floors, at empty skies,
Each heartbeat louder than the last goodbye.
I see your lips move, shaping thoughts untold,
But all that leaves them is the weight of stone.
Your eyes, once bright, now cast in shadowed hues,

No longer reach for mine in love's soft plea.
The room, though filled, feels hollow, distant, cold,
And silence swells until it cracks the air.
I want to speak, to fill the void we've made,
But fear keeps all my words locked tight inside.
And so we sit in silence, side by side,
As if this quiet speaks the truth we hide.

A Love Tested

The storm has come, the sky is torn,
And we, like trees, must bend or break.
For love to last, it must be worn,
But in its cracks, new roots will take.

Cracked Petals

I watched the petals crack beneath your gaze,
Once soft, now brittle, fragile in the air.
Your hands, though gentle, cast a harsher blaze,
And burned away the love we used to wear.
What happened to the days when we were free,
When every touch was like a springtime bloom?
Now every glance is heavy, hard to see,
And silence wraps itself around the room.
The petals fall, one by one,
Cracking softly as they land.

Broken Promises

Our promises, like glass, have shattered wide,
And now we walk on pieces of regret.
Each step we take, the pain we cannot hide,
Reminds us of the vows we can't forget.

Thorns at the Heart

The thorns have twisted tightly round our hearts,
And every beat now bleeds into the air.
We once believed that love could heal the parts,
But now we find the truth too sharp to bear.
The rose we thought would blossom without end,
Now wilts beneath the weight of all we've done.
And though we try, and though we both pretend,
The petals fall, one by one, by one.
Perhaps the thorns were always there, unseen,
Beneath the bloom we held so dear, so fast.
For love, though sweet, is rarely ever clean—
It cuts us deep, and deeper still at last.
And so we stand, our hands both bloodied red,
With love in pieces, broken, cold, and dead.

Fractured Silence

Between us lies a silence cracked and worn,
Each piece a memory we dare not speak.
The words that once fell softly now have turned
To heavy stones that lie beneath our feet.
And though I long to bridge this space again,
The quiet holds me fast, its grip too tight.
Our love, once bright, now fades to shades of gray,
A silent wound that deepens with the night.

Withering Leaves

Our love, like leaves in autumn's cold,
Once vibrant, now begins to fade.
The colors dim, the warmth grows old,
As roots pull back from vows we made.

Splinters

Love's edges, sharp as splintered wood,
Have pricked my heart, and though I bleed,
I find I cannot leave this place—
I'm bound to you by roots and need.
Each tender word has turned to dust,
A brittle song we strain to hear.
Yet in this pain, I feel the trust
That holds me close, despite my fear.

Shadows Cast

I stand in the shadow of our love,
Where light has given way to gray.
Your voice echoes in empty rooms,
A sound I chase, but cannot stay.
What once was warmth has turned to shade,
A presence felt but never near.
Love, in its truest form, endures—
Yet even shadows disappear.

Petals in Ash

The rose we cherished turns to ash,
Its petals blackened by the fire.
Once beautiful, it's lost its flash,
Consumed by pain, by cold desire.

Love's War

Our hearts, like soldiers battle-worn and frayed,
Now struggle in a war that love has made.
With wounds unseen, we press and pull apart,
Each clash a mark upon a fragile heart.

Thorns Beneath the Bloom

Beneath the bloom, the thorns begin to show,
A hidden truth that beauty tries to hide.
In tangled vines, our hearts are left to grow,
With love, now burdened, caught up in its pride.
We hold each other close, though pain remains,
Each touch a prick that cuts beneath the skin.
And though we try to break away these chains,
The deeper wounds have taken root within.
For love is rarely sweet without the sting,
A rose with thorns as fierce as they are fine.
Yet in this pain, a quiet strength takes wing,
As hearts endure, and still, their roots entwine.

Chapter 4
Falling Petals (The End of Love / Letting Go)

Opening Quote:
"Letting go is not the end of love; it is the beginning of grace."
~~ Jaydin Donough

Petals on the Wind

The petals drift like whispers in the wind,
Each one a memory we used to hold.
Once vibrant, they are faded, bruised, and thinned,
No longer bright, no longer rich with gold.
I watch them float away on quiet air,
The weight of loss too gentle to restrain.
And though we once believed our love was rare,
The petals fall, too delicate to remain.
The garden where we bloomed is overgrown,
With weeds and thorns where roses used to stand.
And though the earth beneath our roots has grown,
It's time to walk away with open hands.
For love, though strong, can wither, fade, and part,
But grace is found in every healing heart.

Farewell in Silence

We part in silence, not in blame or spite,
Like fading stars that vanish with the night.

Ballad of a Lost Heart

She stood beside the riverside, her heart no longer bold,
For once, she held his love so close, now love had turned to cold.
The water, dark and running fast, reflected skies of gray,
And in her chest, she felt the past slip quietly away.
He walked alone among the trees, his footsteps soft with care,
For once, his love was all he knew, now loss was in the air.
The leaves beneath his feet were dry, their colors worn and frayed,
And in the silence, he walked by, as all their promises decayed.
For love, though bright, can dim with time, and hearts can lose their flame,
And though they parted without crime, they parted just the same.
The river flows, the trees stand still, but hearts no longer beat,
Together now, they feel the chill of love's forgotten heat.

Soft Goodbyes

Your hand slips from mine, like a leaf in the wind,
Silent and soft, as the autumn begins.
The days grow colder, the skies turn to gray,
And slowly, our love is drifting away.
We tried to hold on, but time had its say,
The edges of us have begun to decay.
No bitterness lingers, no harshness or blame,
Just quiet farewells, like a soft dying flame.
And so, as we part, I will carry this peace,
For even in endings, there's beauty's release.

The Parting Kiss

The parting kiss was soft and sweet,
Like petals falling on the street.
We said goodbye with gentle grace,
No tear was shed, no need to chase.
For though we loved, the time had come,
To let each other move along.
No anger there, no harsh regret,
Just love that we would not forget.
The seasons turn, the winds will blow,
And we, like leaves, will gently go.
But in our hearts, the bloom remains,
A love once held, now free of chains.

The Final Petal

The final petal fell today,
It drifted down without a sound.
I watched it land, then float away,
As love returned to solid ground.
We held on tight, through storm and calm,
Through nights of doubt, through days of bliss.
But in the end, we must disarm,
And say goodbye with one last kiss.
The garden where our love once grew,
Now silent, waits for something new.

Love's Quiet Departure

Love doesn't leave with angry cries,
It simply fades with quiet grace.
A soft goodbye, a glance, a sigh,
And we return to our own space.

Fading Light

The light between us fades with every breath,
A gentle dimming, soft and unafraid.
For love is not extinguished by its death,
But carried on in memories we've made.
The sky is painted hues of fading gold,
As twilight falls upon this love we knew.
And though we've let it slip from fingers cold,
I carry warmth in everything we grew.
So take my hand one final time, my dear,
And let this moment mark a sweet release.
For though the end of love is drawing near,
It leaves behind a quiet, tender peace.
No longer bound by what was meant to be,
We walk away, and finally, we're free.

TALES OF NATURE LOST AMONG THE THORNS

A Breeze Through Empty Branches

A breeze now stirs through empty branches bare,
Where once the leaves of love had softly grown.
I feel the space where warmth was always there,
But now I stand in autumn winds, alone.

Where the River Ends

We followed love's river until it ran dry,
Where once it flowed freely beneath open sky.
The waters grew shallow, the current grew weak,
And soon there was nothing left to seek.
I watched as it narrowed, then faded to sand,
The place where our hearts once walked hand in hand.
And though I had hoped it would carry us far,
The river has ended, and here we are.

Glass and Ashes

We built our love with fragile glass,
Too thin to last, too sharp to hold.
And now it's fallen into ash,
A story burned, too soon, too cold.

Shadows on the Wall

Your shadow lingers still upon the wall,
A faint reminder of the love we lost.
The room, though filled with light, feels empty now,
As though your absence stains the very air.
I reach for you in dreams I cannot hold,
And even when I wake, your name remains—
A ghost, a whisper, hanging on my lips,
A shadow I can never brush away.

Empty Hands

I once held love, but now my hands are bare,
The space between my fingers filled with air.

The Unspoken Goodbye

We never said goodbye, not with our words,
But silence lingered heavy in the air.
A weight that neither of us dared disturb,
Too fragile, and too painful still to bear.
The end was written long before we spoke,
In every quiet glance, in every sigh.
And though our hearts had tangled, they were broke,
Still tied, but waiting patiently to die.
And so we part without a single sound,
No farewell kiss, no words of love's release.
Just empty rooms and echoes all around,
And somewhere, in the stillness, lies our peace.

The Garden Left Behind

The garden where we planted love is bare,
Its flowers wilted, crumbled into dust.
And though the soil still waits, I'm unaware,
If once again, we'll find the strength to trust.

Chapter 5: Rebirth (Healing and New Beginnings)

Opening Quote:
"The beauty of love lies not only in its bloom but in the way it rises again from the roots of loss."
~~Jaydin Donough

New Roots

The ground that once was barren, dry, and cracked,
Now opens wide with shoots of tender green.
Where once my heart had broken, worn and lacked,
New roots have grown where pain has always been.
With every step, I feel the earth below,
Alive with promise, waiting for the sun.
For though the petals of the past may blow,
New life begins when healing has begun.
And here, among the trees that rise and stand,
I plant new seeds, I open up my hand.
For love, like nature, finds its way back home,
Through rain and storm, it blooms where it has grown.

Soft Rain

The rain falls softly on my skin,
Each drop a reminder that life still flows.
The air is thick with the scent of earth,
Damp and alive,
As the ground opens wide to drink it in.
I stand beneath the silver sky,
Feeling the weight of every drop—
Not as a burden,
But as a gift.
For in the rain, I find release.
Each drop washing away
The dust of what was,
The pain of what no longer is.
And in its place,
A quiet peace settles.

Love Returns

In the softest light of dawn,
Love returns like a gentle breeze,
Stirring the leaves that once lay still,
Breathing life into the quiet trees.
The sky, once gray, now blushing bright,
And with it comes the morning's grace.
For though love once had taken flight,
It finds its way back to this place.

The Dawn of Us

With dawn comes light,
With light comes hope,
And with hope, love finds its way once more.
The darkest night had closed me in,
But now the sky is wide and clear.
The stars have faded, one by one,
As sunlight stretches, golden, dear.
And in this light, I find my heart,
Awakened from the long, cold night.
For though the past may weigh me down,
I rise again, bathed in this light.

Budding Again

In the space where love once bloomed and died,
A new bud forms—small,
But full of promise.
The soil is soft beneath my feet,
Rich with the remnants of what was.
But now, it is not weighed down by loss.
Instead, it feeds the roots of what will be.
I bend down to touch the tender bud,
Fingers grazing its delicate leaves.
And in this quiet, I know—
Love is never truly lost,
It simply transforms,
And buds again.

The Light of Healing

The light of healing shines within,
Where broken hearts can bloom again.

The Rise of Love
)

From ashes grows the sweetest bloom,
From broken hearts, new life will start.
For love is born in every room,
Where once there was an empty heart.

Roots that reach

The roots of love grow deep beneath the soil,
Invisible, but strong in every way.
Though storms may come and years may often toil,
These roots remain, and quietly they stay.
When love once lost begins to bud anew,
It reaches deep, beneath what's torn and weak.
The branches rise, the leaves drink in the dew,
And love returns, no longer soft or meek.
For strength is found in what we cannot see,
In what is felt beneath the ground we tread.
And though the past may bend us to our knee,
The roots of love sustain what we once said.
So now we rise, with every leaf in bloom,
A garden grown where once there was no room.

A Heart Replanted

I've planted love within my chest,
Its roots now reaching far and wide.
And in my heart, I feel it rest,
A bloom reborn, no need to hide.

The Garden Reclaimed

The garden once abandoned blooms again,
With flowers rich and full, where weeds once grew.
The soil, once cracked and dry beneath the rain,
Is soft and rich, a place where love renews.
And though the thorns still linger on the vine,
Their sharpness cannot steal the beauty here.
For love, once found, will always realign,
And even in its loss, it reappears.

Chapter 6: Traditional Love

Opening Quote:
"True love is not found in fleeting passion, but in the quiet moments of loyalty and devotion."
~~Jaydin Donough

Of Vows and Rings
(Heroic Couplets)

In golden vows, we bind our hearts as one,
Through trials faced, we vow to never run.
This ring, a circle perfect and complete,
Is love's embrace that makes our lives replete.
Through every storm, we stand in steadfast grace,
For love, in time, will never lose its place.
No greater bond than this that we now share,
A lifelong promise, tender as a prayer.

Courtship
(Shakespearean Sonnet)

Our courtship bloomed beneath a setting sun,
With stolen glances, words of soft desire.
And as the stars above our heads were spun,
Our hearts were lit with love's eternal fire.
Each tender look, a promise unspoken,
Each brush of hands, a spark that soon would grow.
And in the silence, vows remained unbroken,
For love, though young, was all we came to know.
The days have passed, and still we walk this path,
With every step, our bond has only grown.
Through all of time, I'll honor love's sweet math—
Two hearts made one, forever we have sown.
So let us walk, with hands entwined in light,
For love will guide us gently through the night.

Bound by Tradition
(Quatrain, abab)
We walk the road that many hearts have known,
A path where love is built with steady hands.
No need for wild desire, we have grown,
Within the rules that history demands.

A Marriage of Hearts
(Heroic Couplets)
A marriage of two hearts that beat as one,
A sacred bond that time has just begun.
With every step, we grow within this place,
Where love and loyalty find equal grace.
Through all the years, this vow will never break,
For love like ours, no storms will ever shake.
Our hands entwined, our futures set in stone,
Together, we will build a life well-known.

The Promise
(Spenserian Sonnet)
In quiet moments, when the world stands still,
I hear your heartbeat echoing with mine.
This promise made, I vow to always fill
Your life with love, as steady as the vine.
The seasons pass, and yet our love remains,
Unchanging like the stars that grace the skies.
Though time may try to shift our joy to pains,
I see forever glowing in your eyes.
For love, when built with trust and open hands,
Is stronger than the storms that fill our days.
And as we stand upon this blessed land,
I know our hearts will never lose their ways.
So here I stand, my hand within your own,
Forever bound by love that we have grown.

The Family Tree
(Quatrain, abab)
We planted love as roots beneath the earth,
And from our bond, a family has grown.
Each branch that spreads is testament to worth,
A life that's shared, and never walked alone.

Love's Steadfast Flame
(Lyric Poem)
The flame of love burns bright, but steady still,
Through every day, it flickers in the dark.
Not wild, not reckless, but with quiet will,
It lights the path we've walked from love's first spark.
In every moment, I feel its warm embrace,
A fire that glows but never seeks to burn.
For love, in time, will never lose its place,
And to its steady warmth, we always turn.

Legacy of Love
(Quatrain, abab)
Our love will last beyond the years we know,
A legacy of all that we have built.
Through every life, our story's light will grow,
For love, like water, never stays unspilt.

In Your Hands
(Couplet)

In your hands, I place my life, my trust,
For love is built on hands that hold, not thrust.

Through the Years
(Sonnet)

Through all the years, our love will stand in time,
A testament to what is good and true.
For every season, joy or pain, or climb,
I vow to walk this path of life with you.
Our youth may fade, our hair may turn to gray,
But love will never wane or lose its grace.
And when the world has turned to yesterday,
I'll hold you still, with hands that time can't chase.
For love, when real, will never need the light,
It burns within, unseen by passing days.
And though the years may take away our sight,
Our hearts will guide us through the cloudy haze.
So walk with me, through all the years to come,
For in your arms, my heart will rest, be home.

Chapter 7: Modern Love

Opening Quote:
"Love is no longer confined to definitions; it grows where it pleases, untamed and unafraid."
~~Jaydin Donough

Unwritten Rules
(Free Verse)
We love without the need for maps or guides,
Tracing our own constellations in the sky.
Who needs to follow the rules,
When love makes its own path?
Your hand in mine,
But never gripping too tight,
We walk side by side,
Unbound by what love "should" be.
No contracts, no promises,
Just the understanding that we are enough,
In this moment,
In this space.

Self-Love
(Prose Poem)

I look in the mirror and see a reflection not of what I should be, but of who I am. There's beauty in the imperfections, in the flaws that once made me hide. I don't need love from outside to feel whole. I am the ocean, vast and deep, and the waves that crash against my shore are my own—pushing and pulling with the tides of my own heart.

In this moment, I belong to no one but myself, and that is enough.

Love Without Labels
(Free Verse)
You and I,
We never needed a label to define us.
Why box love into a word
When it's meant to spill over the edges?
Your laugh, my touch,
They speak more than any word could.
We exist in a space all our own,
Not lovers, not friends—
Just two souls in sync.
The world may ask, "What are you?"
But we smile,
Knowing that what we are
Is beyond definition.

Breaking the Mold
(Free Verse)
We broke the mold the day we met.
No script to follow,
No guidebook to tell us what's next.
Just two hearts, untethered,
Finding their own rhythm.
Our love doesn't fit into any box—
It bends, twists, expands.
Some days, it's soft like the morning light,
Other days, it's fierce, a storm of passion.
But through it all,
It's real.
It's ours.

The Heart's Freedom
(Prose Poem)

There's a freedom in this love—one that breathes with ease, never suffocated by expectation or need. We don't own each other. We don't chain ourselves to words like "forever."

Instead, we love in the here and now, unburdened by tomorrow or yesterday. Your heart is yours, and mine is mine, but when we come together, something new is created—something that doesn't ask for anything but the moment.

Love, in this form, is an open sky, and we are birds flying free.

Love Unbound
(Free Verse)
Our love is a river,
Flowing where it pleases.
Sometimes it's deep and slow,
Carving through the rock,
Other times it's wild,
Rushing past the banks.
There are no dams to hold it back,
No walls to keep it contained.
We let it move,
Unbound,
Free.

The Space Between
(Quatrain, abab)
The space between us speaks so loud,
A silence full of choice.
No need for chains, no need for vows,
Just trust within our voice.

Fluid Love
(Lyric Poem)
Our love is fluid,
It shifts and sways,
Dancing to rhythms
That change with the days.
Some nights, it's a whisper,
A soft, gentle touch,
Other times, it's a river,
And it asks for so much.
But no matter the form
That it chooses to take,
We know in our hearts
That this love will not break.

A Love That Grows
(Free Verse)
We grow together,
But not in the same direction.
You reach for the sun,
While I stretch toward the moon.
And somehow,
We meet in the middle,
Where light and dark embrace,
Where opposites find their peace.

Beyond Expectations
(Prose Poem)

We don't live by anyone's rules but our own. Love doesn't need a checklist, a timeline, or a goal. It simply is. We exist beyond the expectations of the world, beyond the need to explain or define. What we have is ours—raw, real, imperfect, and that's what makes it beautiful.

There's no pressure here, no demands. Just love in its purest form, free from the weight of tradition.

Chapter 8: Spiritual Love (Transcendence)

Opening Quote:
"Love, in its truest form, transcends the body and touches the soul, connecting us to something greater."
~~Jaydin Donough

The Soul's Embrace
(Ode)
In quiet moments, when the world stands still,
I feel your spirit woven into mine.
A love that breathes beyond the body's will,
Transcendent, sacred, bound by the divine.
No words are needed here in this embrace,
No touch required to feel your presence near.
For love exists beyond both time and space,
An echo of the stars that we hold dear.
And even when the world begins to fade,
Our souls will dance beneath the endless sky.
For love, when true, will never be afraid
To rise again, no matter how we die.

Divine Love
(Lyric Poem)

There is a love that flows like light,
From heart to heart, from soul to soul.
It moves through time, beyond our sight,
A love that makes the broken whole.
It whispers in the quiet dawn,
And wraps around the darkest night.
It lives in every breath we draw,
A love divine, both pure and bright.

Eternal Threads
(Ode)

Our love is woven deep within the stars,
An unseen thread that binds us, heart to heart.
Though miles and years may stretch our souls apart,
The universe will never break these bars.
For in the quiet hum of every night,
I hear your voice, a whisper in the dark.
It carries me like stardust, soft and bright,
A light that guides me home, a cosmic spark.
And even when the day begins to fade,
When all we know returns to endless space,
This thread will hold, unbreakable and strong,
For love, eternal, carries on its song.

Whispers of the Infinite
(Lyric Poem)
In the stillness, I hear your voice,
A whisper from the infinite.
It flows through time, a gentle choice,
And in its song, I find my fit.
Your love is like a breeze at dawn,
Softly stirring, barely seen.
And though the night may stretch too long,
I feel you near, in all between.

Self-Love, Eternal
(Couplet)
In silence, I have found my heart,
A love eternal from the start.

Love Unseen
(Ode)

Your love, though unseen, surrounds me still,
A force that wraps me tight in light.
It carries me through every hill,
A hand that guides me through the night.
I feel it in the wind that blows,
In every star, in every tree.
It lives in all that nature grows,
An energy that sets me free.
For love, though hidden from the eye,
Is felt within the deepest soul.
It moves beneath the quiet sky,
And makes the broken heart feel whole.

The Universe's Pulse
(Lyric Poem)
I hear the pulse of the universe,
A rhythm steady, calm, and sure.
It beats within my heart and yours,
A song that stretches evermore.
In every wave, in every breath,
The universe hums love's refrain.
And though the world may move to death,
This pulse of love will still remain.

In the Light of Love
(Couplet)
In love's soft light, I find my way,
Through every night and endless day.

Cosmic Dance
(Ode)

We dance beneath a sky of endless stars,
Our souls entwined in rhythms deep and true.
Each step we take, the universe regards,
A cosmic waltz that only we two knew.
The planets move in harmony with us,
The stars a witness to our endless grace.
For love, when joined by souls that dare to trust,
Becomes a dance no force can dare erase.
And even when the music starts to fade,
Our dance will carry on through time and space.
For love, when born within the soul's bright core,
Will live beyond the heavens evermore.

Prayers of Love
(Lyric Poem)
I send my prayers of love to you,
A wish upon the wind so high.
It carries whispers soft and true,
And floats beyond the open sky.
My love for you, though far apart,
Lives deep within my every prayer.
For though you're gone, you're in my heart,
A love that waits for me somewhere.

Inner Peace
(Ode)

Within the quiet corners of my heart,
I find the peace that only love can bring.
A peace that soothes the broken, torn apart,
A gentle hand that mends my every wing.
For love, when known within, is strong and true,
A force that cannot wither, break, or bend.
It carries me through all I say and do,
A peace that holds me, faithful to the end.

TALES OF NATURE LOST AMONG THE THORNS

Hearts of the Stars
(Lyric Poem)
The stars above, they speak our name,
Their light a mirror of our soul.
For love like ours is just the same,
Eternal, bright, and ever whole.

Conclusion: The Circle of Love
(Narrative or Ode)

Love blooms in every season of the heart,
From tender bud to vibrant, full display.
It takes its roots in joy, yet plays its part
In grief and loss, in all that fades away.
For love is not a single, steady thing—
It bends, it breaks, it heals, it grows anew.
It carries us on fragile, trembling wing,
And in its flight, it shows us what is true.
The early blush of love is soft and bright,
A rose just born beneath the springtime sun.
But soon the thorns appear, the petals light
Begin to fall, their fleeting beauty done.
Yet even as the bloom begins to fade,
A seed is left to grow within the soil.
And through the darkest nights, we are remade,
Our hearts reborn from every tear and toil.
For love, though bruised, will always find its way,
Through storm and silence, through the weight of time.
It whispers in the night and lights the day,
A circle spinning, endless and sublime.
So as we end this tale of rose and thorn,
We know that love is never truly lost.
For in its fall, another bud is born,
And every heart must bear both bloom and cost.
We walk through love—its beauty and its pain,
Embracing all it brings, both sweet and sad.
For love, like rain, must fall and rise again,
And in its circle, we are whole and glad.

Epilogue

"At 19 years old, I'll admit I haven't yet experienced love in all its deepest forms. But writing this book has given me a space to reflect, to look inward, and to try and understand what love might feel like in all its beauty and complexity. Through each poem, I took a journey into introspection, discovering how love—its joy, pain, and transformation—has the power to change us.

While I might still be at the beginning of understanding it, I hope these poems offer you a glimpse into love's deepest beauty and strength. This book taught me that love is both a force and a journey, something worth waiting for, worth growing through, and worth experiencing in every way possible."

Notes

"Tales of Nature Lost Among the Thorns explores love in its most profound and layered forms, yet it also connects to my previous work, Please Don't Forget About Me, my second book.
In Please Don't Forget About Me, I dedicated every poem to someone I haven't met yet, someone who I hope will know that I've been waiting for her all along. The themes in Tales of Nature Lost Among the Thorns extend from that dedication. While Please Don't Forget About Me captured the longing and waiting, this collection dives into the essence of love itself—its roots, blooms, and, yes, its thorns. Through both books, I hope to express love's power to shape us, both in presence and absence, and how it connects us across time and experience.*"

Final Message

"Thank you for reading Tales of Nature Lost Among the Thorns. May these poems remind you of the beauty in both the joy and challenges of love, and may you find strength in its cycles of growth and renewal. Whether love feels close or far, know that it's a force that continues to shape and guide us all. Here's to embracing each petal and thorn along the way, and to all the paths that love will continue to unfold in your life."

Symbols

Thorns: Symbolize the pain and challenges that often accompany love, the moments of conflict, or personal growth.
Petals: Represent the beauty and fragility of love in its purest form, highlighting the gentleness and tenderness in each stage of the journey.
Rebirth: The stage in love and life where one finds new strength and purpose, emerging stronger after loss or hardship.

Glossary for Readers

Affection: A gentle feeling of fondness or love for someone, often shown through kind actions or words.

Barren: Empty or lacking life; often describes land with no plants, but can also mean a heart that feels lonely or empty.

Bound: Tied or connected to something or someone, often with a strong commitment or love.

Confession: Sharing a truth or feeling, often about love or emotions that are difficult to express.

Cradle: To hold something gently, like holding a baby, often used to describe caring for someone with love.

Desire: A strong feeling of wanting something or someone, especially in a romantic or emotional way.

Ember: A small piece of burning coal or wood that stays hot after a fire; often symbolizes a lasting, hidden feeling.

Eternal: Lasting forever; used to describe feelings, such as love, that feel endless.

Faded: Something that has lost color or strength, like old memories or feelings that are slowly disappearing.

Frail: Weak or delicate, often describing something fragile that needs gentle care.

Gaze: A soft or intense look; in poetry, a gaze often expresses love, admiration, or longing.

Gentle: Soft and kind; describes how someone might act with love or compassion.

Glimmer: A small, flickering light, often used to symbolize hope or a small, bright feeling.

Grief: Deep sadness, usually because of loss or heartbreak.

Hollow: Empty inside; used to describe feelings of loneliness or emptiness after loss.

Horizon: The line where the earth and sky meet; often symbolizes distant dreams, goals, or future possibilities.

Innocence: A state of purity or not yet knowing hurt; often describes love that is new, pure, and untested by hardship.

Intimate: Close and personal; describes a deep connection between people, often involving trust and affection.

Lingering: Something that stays for a long time, like a scent, feeling, or memory.

Longing: A deep desire for something or someone, often associated with yearning or missing a person.

Nestled: Comfortably placed or settled, like being safe in someone's arms or feeling protected.

Nurture: To care for someone or something, helping it grow, like nurturing a relationship.

Presence: Being there with someone, either physically or emotionally; can also refer to feeling someone's spirit nearby.

Pulse: The beat of a heart; in poetry, it often symbolizes life, love, or emotion that is alive within.

Quietude: A state of calm or peace; often describes a moment of stillness, where one feels at ease or reflective.

Resilient: Able to withstand or recover from hardship; often used to describe people who stay strong through challenges.

Sacred: Something considered holy or deeply respected, often used to describe the bond between two people in love.

Sever: To cut off or break, often describing the end of a connection or relationship.

Sigh: A deep breath often expressing emotion, like relief, sadness, or longing.

Silent: Completely without sound, often used in poetry to describe moments of introspection, peace, or loneliness.

Solace: Comfort given during times of sadness or distress.

Stillness: A lack of movement or noise; often symbolizes peace, reflection, or the quiet moments in a relationship.

Tethered: Bound or connected to someone or something; can refer to an emotional attachment that holds people together.

Transcend: To go beyond normal limits; often describes feelings that are spiritual or deeply profound.

Tremble: A slight shaking, often due to strong emotions like excitement, fear, or love.

Unfurl: To open up or spread out, like a flower blooming or emotions being revealed.

Unseen: Something hidden or not visible, often describing emotions or connections that aren't physically obvious.

Vessel: A container or carrier; in poetry, it can mean the body as a vessel for emotions or love.

Whisper: To speak softly; in poetry, whispers are often symbols of secrets, love, or gentle communication.

Yearn: To want something deeply, often something that feels just out of reach.

Through Different Eyes: Personal Views on Love

Jaydin

"I think of love as a philosophical idea, something rooted deeply in spiritual beliefs. Scriptures say 'God is love, and whoever abides in God abides in love.' To me, love is like a yin and yang—after spiritual love, self-love is vital. It's in the commandments: love God, love yourself, and love your neighbor. Without self-love, it's hard to truly love others.

Love, like yin and yang, flows like a river. It can take any shape, but it can't be contained. Love is gentle, kind, patient, and it's the foundation of life. Yet, it's become so over-cliched that we sometimes miss its true depth."

Leah

"I don't really think love's real anymore. I've been hurt too many times. I know it's real for some people, but finding your soulmate the first time—that's rare. In the past, love for me was just a feeling based on my partner's actions and words. My whole mood depended on them."

Matthew

"Love isn't a feeling; it's a choice. It's deciding to be there, even when things aren't easy."

Zeenat

"It's not a word; more of an action or a memory. Love is so many things woven together—not just happiness, but the feeling you get around a certain person. It can bring out so many emotions and trigger different feelings, and that's what makes it beautiful. Everyone has a different idea of love, some more alike than others. Love can be beautiful, but it can also hurt and tear people apart or bring them closer. But I can tell you this—it isn't something you should chase. It's something you should be patient about, and it will find you. Love is about patience, not forcing it."

Kate

"Love is real in both its emotional and physical way."

Musfeeka

"Love, to me, is something felt only between two people who truly feel something for each other. It's an emotion that's indescribable. You can't see it, but you feel it. It comes from the inner soul."

Aiden

"I won't give a long story. For me, it's when two worlds come together and make one planet, you know what I mean?"

Fatima

"I don't know, to be honest. But if I had to say, love would be a mutual understanding between oneself and one's partner. It's about respect, dignity, honor, love, hate, possessiveness, passion, consent—all that should be in a relationship. It's okay to argue sometimes, but there's a boundary that shouldn't be crossed."

Haylin

"I've never been in a relationship before. But from what I've seen and heard, love is real—it depends on the person or thing, though. I could say 'I love you' hypothetically, but it might just be a flimsy feeling. And then, I could say 'I love you' to someone I've known for a long time, and it would mean something sincere. There's a difference in the 'I love you's.' I think love is the most honest, purest, and scariest thing that exists in life. But, if I'm being honest, I don't believe in love, because it changes people. Love, to me, means change. And I'm afraid of change."

Rashieda

"I do think love is real, and yes, it's a feeling, I guess. I can't say I've experienced being in love romantically, but it's a feeling I'd describe as 'captivating.' When I fall in love, I want it to be a feeling that makes me happy, safe, and appreciated. Even though I haven't experienced it, I know it's something that should mean a lot. That's why I'm glad I don't date just anyone. When I do, I want it to be with someone I'm giving my heart to for the rest of my life."

Nafeesa

"Love is having respect for each other, showing support, going the extra mile. Love is also about making each other happy and accepting each other's flaws."

Also by Silent writer

Tales of Nature Lost among the Thorns

Watch for more at www.wattpad.

Also by Jaydin C Donough

Please Don't Forget About Me Tea For My Soul
Tales of Nature Lost among the Thorns